The Gift of Friendship

A friend is a rare book,
of which but one copy is made.
—Author Unknown

IDEALS PUBLICATIONS INCORPORATED

NASHVILLE, TENNESSEE

Friendship is the most precious of flowers
that grow in the garden of life.
Author Unknown

ACKNOWLEDGMENTS

THE FRIENDLY WAY from *THE FRIENDLY WAY* by Edgar A. Guest, copyright ©1931 by The Reilly & Lee Co., used by permission of the author's estate. LINES FOR A FRIEND'S HOUSE from *THE LIGHT OF FAITH* by Edgar A. Guest, copyright ©1926 by The Reilly & Lee Co., used by permission of the author's estate. LIVING WITH THE PEOPLE from *THE PASSING THRONG* by Edgar A. Guest, copyright ©1923 by The Reilly & Lee Co., used by permission of the author's estate. WHEN YOU KNOW A FELLOW from *A HEAP O' LIVIN'* by Edgar A. Guest, copyright ©1916 by The Reilly & Britton Co., used by permission of the author's estate. SHAKE HANDS from *THE COLLECTED POEMS OF A. E. HOUSMAN*. Copyright ©1939, 1940 by Henry Holt and Co., Inc. Copyright ©1967 by Robert E. Symons. Reprinted by permission of Henry Holt and Co., Inc. and the Society of Authors as the literary representative of the estate of A. E. Housman. LIFELONG FRIENDS from *FIRESIDE POEMS* by Edna Jaques, published in Canada by Thomas Allen & Son Limited. IN THE FOREST from *THE ROUND OF THE YEAR* by Patience Strong, copyright ©1948 by E. P. Dutton & Co. Reprinted by permission of Rupert Crew Limited. TIME SIFTS OUR FRIENDSHIPS by Patience Strong, from *THE FRIENDSHIP BOOK*, published 1962 by Frederick Muller Ltd. Reprinted by permission of Rupert Crew Limited. AROUND THE CORNER from *SELECTED POEMS* by Charles Hanson Towne, copyright 1925 by D. Appleton & Co., copyright renewed 1953 by Ara Searle. Used by permission of Dutton, a division of Penguin Books USA Inc. Our sincere thanks to the following authors whom we were unable to contact: Abbie Farwell Brown for FRIENDS, Elsie M. Farr for FRIENDS THROUGH CORRESPONDENCE, Francis J. Gable for FRIENDSHIP, Carleton Everett Knox for I FOUND LOVELINESS TODAY, Pat Lassen for THE HEART OF A FRIEND, Sarah Litsey for ALL CHILDREN SCUFF THE LEAVES, James J. Metcalfe for ANOTHER FRIEND and FRIENDLY THINGS, Wilbur D. Nesbit for A FRIEND OR TWO, Lea Palmer for THE EVER-OPEN DOOR, Adam N. Reiter for TO AN OLD FRIEND'S HOUSE, Edwin Roworth for LIFE'S RIPPLES, Elizabeth Selden for SONG OF NATURE, Harry Halsey Starrett for THE TRUE FRIEND, and B. Y. Williams for THE FRIEND WHO JUST STANDS BY.

Editor, Nancy J. Skarmeas; Copy Editor, Michelle Prater Burke; Electronic Prepress, Amilyn K. Lanning

Printed and bound in the U.S.A.

ISBN 0-8249-4070-9

Designed by Gore Studio, Inc.
Film separations by WebTech Inc.
Printed by R.R. Donnelly & Sons, Inc.

Contents

The Nature of Friendship

Friends

If you had all the lands and gold
    It's possible for man to hold,
And if on top of that could claim
    The greatest sum of earthly fame,
Yet had to live from day to day
    Where never human came your way,
You'd trade the gold you had to spend
    To hear the greeting of a friend.

What joy can come from splendid deeds
    That no one ever cheers or heeds?
Fame would be empty and absurd
    If of it no one ever heard.

The richest man, without a friend,
    Is poor with all he has to spend.
Alone, with all that could be had,
    Each one of us would still be sad.

Not in ourselves does fortune lie,
    Nor in the things that gold can buy;
The words of praise that please so well
    The lips of other men must tell.
And honor, on which joy depends,
    Is but the verdict of our friends.
All happiness that man can know
    The friends about him must bestow.

—Author Unknown

A friend is a present you give yourself.

Robert Louis Stevenson

Life's Ripples

A tiny pebble idly tossed
Into the placid stream,
With gentle splash it sinks from sight
And not again is seen.
But outward from that central spot
The circling ripples tend;
Who knows on what far distant shore
The spreading impulse ends?

And so it is with life itself;
A kind thing we say or do
May take a moment of our time
And then be lost to view.
But ever onward it will go
And never lost shall be
Until its widening mission done,
It joins infinity.

—Edwin Roworth

Reward of Service

The sweetest lives are those to
  duty wed,
Whose deeds both great and small
Are close-knit strands of an unbroken
  thread
Where love ennobles all.
The world may sound no trumpets,
  ring no bells;
The Book of Life the slurring record
  tells.

Thy love shall chant its own beatitudes
After its own like working. A child's kiss
Set on thy singing lips shall make
  thee glad;
A poor man served by thee shall make
  thee rich;
A sick man helped by thee shall make
  thee strong;
Thou shalt be served thyself by every sense
Of service which thou renderest.

—Elizabeth Barrett Browning

Key to Friendship

The real key to friendship
Is a tender, gentle blend
Of this plain and simple truth—
That one must be a friend.

Friendship is based upon
What we give, not what we take,
And it steers its kindly course
For a special friend's own sake.

Friendship which shall endure
And shall never crave an end
Is built upon this truth—
That one must be a friend.

—Edith H. Shank

If a man does not make new
acquaintances as he advances
through life, he will soon find
himself alone. A man, sir,
should keep his friendships in
constant repair.

Samuel Johnson

The Ever-Open Door

What shall I bestow upon a friend? Gay laughter to sustain when sorrow may bring pain, a bright song of life, a belief that winter ends in the glory of spring, and a prayer of hope for peace that will forever stay.

What shall I bestow upon a friend? Songs from my heart which I've hidden away, friendship that flowers once it enters the heart, spring's eternal loveliness, and knowledge that love is a precious thing.

What shall I bestow upon a friend? Fleeting moments of silent blessings; trust in tomorrow, which is life's hardest task; faith that each new dawn brings daylight's golden pathway to the ever-open door; and a belief that God will be with them though all others go their own way.

—Lea Palmer

I give you my love more precious than money;
I give you myself before preaching or law.
Will you give me yourself?
Will you come travel with me?
Shall we stick by each other as long as we live?

Walt Whitman

Around the Corner

Around the corner I have a friend
In this great city that has no end.
Yet days go by and weeks rush on,
And before I know it, a year is gone;
And I never see my old friend's face,
For life is a swift and terrible race.
He knows I like him just as well
As in the days when I rang his bell
And he rang mine.

We were younger then,
And now we are busy, tired men:
Tired with playing a foolish game,
Tired with trying to make a name.

"Tomorrow," I say, "I will call on Jim,
Just to show that I am thinking of him."
But tomorrow comes,
    and tomorrow goes,
And the distance between us
    grows and grows.

Around the corner!—Yet miles away . . .
"Here's a telegram, sir."
    "*Jim died today.*"

And that's what we get
    and deserve in the end:
Around the corner, a vanished friend.

—Charles Hanson Towne

*D*o not keep the alabaster boxes of your love and tenderness sealed until your friends are dead. Fill their lives with sweetness. Speak approving, cheering words while their ears can hear them and while their hearts can be thrilled by them.

Henry Ward Beecher

Time Is Short

You who are letting miserable misunderstandings
run on from year to year,
meaning to clear them up someday;
you who are keeping wretched quarrels alive because you cannot quite
make up your mind that now is the day to sacrifice your pride and kill them;
you who are passing men sullenly on the street, not speaking to them
out of some silly spite, and yet knowing that it would fill you with shame
and remorse if you heard that one of those men were dead tomorrow morning;
you who are letting your neighbor starve
till you hear that he is dying of starvation;
or letting your friend's heart ache
for a word of appreciation or sympathy,
which you mean to give him someday;
if you only could know and see and feel, all of a sudden,
that "the time is short," how it would break the spell!
How you would go instantly and do the thing
which you might never have another chance to do.

—Phillips Brooks

*Though I speak with the tongues of men and of angels,
and have not charity, I am become as sounding brass,
or a tinkling cymbal.
And though I have the gift of prophecy,
and understand all mysteries, and all knowledge;
and though I have all faith,
so that I could remove mountains,
and have not charity, I am nothing.*

I Corinthians 13:1-2

The Excitement of Friendship

Friendship requires that there be an open channel between friends, but it does not demand that that channel be the deepest in our nature. It may be of the shallowest kind and yet the friendship be the truest. For all the different traits of our nature must get their airing through friends, the trivial as well as the significant. We let ourselves out piecemeal it seems, so that only with a host of varied friends can we express ourselves to the fullest. Each friend calls out some particular trait in us, and it requires the whole chorus fitly to teach us what we are. This is the imperative need of friendship. A man with few friends is only half developed; there are whole sides of his nature which are locked up and have never been expressed. He cannot unlock himself; he cannot even discover them; friends alone can stimulate him and open them. Such a man is in prison; his soul is in penal solitude. A man must get friends as he would get food and drink for nourishment and sustenance. And he must keep them, as he would keep his health and wealth, as the infallible safeguards against misery and poverty of spirit.

—Randolph Bourne

While Such Friends Are Near Us

Those are red-letter days in our lives when we meet people who thrill us like a fine poem, people whose handshakes are brimful of unspoken sympathy and whose sweet, rich natures impart to our eager, impatient spirits a wonderful restlessness which, in its essence, is divine.

The perplexities, irritations, and worries that have absorbed us pass like unpleasant dreams, and we wake to see with new eyes and hear with new ears the beauty and harmony of God's real world. The solemn nothings that fill our everyday life blossom suddenly into bright possibilities.

In a word, while such friends are near us we feel that all is well. Perhaps we never saw them before and they may never cross our life's path again; but the influence of their calm, mellow natures is a libation poured upon our discontent, and we feel its healing touch as the ocean feels the mountain stream freshening its brine.

—Helen Keller

The House by the Side of the Road

There are hermit souls that
    live withdrawn
In the peace of their self-content;
There are souls like stars that
    dwell apart
In a fellowless firmament;
There are pioneer souls that
    blaze their paths
Where highways never ran—
But let me live by the side of the road
And be a friend to man.

Let me live in a house by the side
    of the road
Where the race of men go by—
The men who are good and the men
    who are bad,
As good and bad as I.
I would not sit in the scorner's seat
Or hurl the cynic's ban—
Let me live in the house by the side
    of the road
And be a friend to man.

I see from the house by the side
    of the road,
By the side of the highway of life,
The men who press with ardor of hope,
The men who are faint with the strife.
But I turn not away from their smiles
    nor their tears,
Both parts of an infinite plan—
Let me live in the house by the
    side of the road
And be a friend to man.

I know there are brook-gladdened
    meadows ahead
And mountains of wearisome height;
That the road passes on through
    the long afternoon
And stretches away to the night.
And still I rejoice when the
    travelers rejoice
And weep with the strangers that moan
As I live in my house by the side of the road
And be a friend to man.

—Sam Walter Foss

That's a Friend

One whose grip is a little tighter,
One whose smile is a little brighter,
One whose deeds are a little whiter,
   That's what I call a friend.

One who'll lend as quick as he'll borrow,
One who's the same today as tomorrow,
One who'll share your joy and sorrow,
   That's what I call a friend.

One whose thoughts are a little cleaner,
One whose mind is a little keener,
One who avoids those things
      that are meaner,
   That's what I call a friend.

One, when you're gone, who'll miss
      you sadly,

One who'll welcome you back again
      gladly,
One who, though angered, will not
      speak madly,
   That's what I call a friend.

One who is always willing to aid you,
One whose advice has always paid you,
One who defended when others
      flayed you,
   That's what I call a friend.

One who was fine when life
      seemed rotten,
One whose ideals you have not forgotten,
One who has given you more than
      he's gotten,
   That's what I call a friend.

—John Burroughs

A friend may well be reckoned the masterpiece of nature.

Ralph Waldo Emerson

Our Childhood Friends

Early Friendships

Our early friendships never fade,
    Nor do they split from wear.
The threads from which these
        bonds are made
    Are memories we share.

Those memories contain a strength
    Akin to strength of youth
That, as the years increase in length,
    Intensifies this truth.

Much sharper to the aging eye
    Are trials a long time spent.
Much clearer are the days gone by
    With laughter lightly lent

Than what is going on right now
    When problems posed
        are real
And time's too hurried to allow
    The furrowed brow to feel.

We may not meet or clasp the hand
    Or even ply the pen,
But still we're sure folks understand
    Who knew us way back when

Because there pulls a tighter tie
    To old friends than to new;
And they'll agree and tell you why:
    They share those memories too.

—Margaret Rorke

There is magic in the memory of
schoolboy friendships; it softens
the heart and even affects the
nervous system of those who have
no heart.

Benjamin Disraeli

Friends

How good to lie a little while
And look up through the trees!
The sky is like a kind, big smile
Bent sweetly over me.

The sunshine flickers through the lace
Of leaves above my head
And kisses me upon the face
Like Mother before bed.

The wind comes stealing o'er the grass
To whisper pretty things;
And though I cannot see him pass,
I feel his careful wings.

So many gentle friends are near
Whom one can scarcely see;
A child should never feel a fear
Wherever he may be.

—Abbie Farwell Brown

The Unseen Playmate

When children are playing alone on the green,
In comes the playmate that never was seen.
When children are happy and lonely and good,
The Friend of the Children comes
    out of the wood.

Nobody heard him and nobody saw;
His is a picture you never could draw.
But he's sure to be present, abroad or at home,
When children are happy and playing alone.

He lies in the laurels, he runs on the grass,
He sings when you tinkle the musical glass;
Whene'er you are happy and cannot tell why,
The Friend of the Children is sure to be by!

He loves to be little, he hates to be big,
'Tis he that inhabits the caves that you dig;
'Tis he when you play with your soldiers of tin
That sides with the Frenchmen and never can win.

'Tis he, when at night you go off to your bed,
Bids you go to your sleep and not trouble
    your head;
For wherever they're lying, in cupboard or shelf,
'Tis he who will take care of your
    playthings himself!

—Robert Louis Stevenson

We Two Boys Together Clinging

We two boys together clinging,
One the other never leaving,
Up and down the roads going, north and south excursions making,
Power enjoying, elbows stretching, fingers clutching,
Arm'd and fearless, eating, drinking, sleeping, loving,
No law less than ourselves owning, sailing, soldiering, thieving,
    threatening,
Misers, menials, priests alarming, air breathing, water drinking, on
    the turf or the sea-beach dancing,
Cities wrenching, ease scorning, statutes mocking, feebleness chasing,
Fulfilling our foray.

—Walt Whitman

Sisters

For there is no friend like a sister
In calm or stormy weather;
To cheer one on the tedious way,
To fetch one if one goes astray,
To lift one if one totters down,
To strengthen whilst one stands.

—Christina Rossetti

Mother of a Boy, Age Three

If you have left a work you planned
To take a small child by the hand
And walk with him where flowers grow
Or play with him there in the snow

Or read his favorite story o'er
Though you have read it oft before
Or help him fly a kite up high
Or find a nest where bird eggs lie;

If you have answered countless why's
And viewed the world through
    a child's eyes
And helped him see the good to do
That he would grow up kind and true;

If you have left your easy chair
To listen to a small child's prayer
And with a hug you've tucked him in
And said a little prayer for him,
Then you are what a mom should be,
The mother of a boy, age three.

—Kay Hoffman

Early Friendship

The half-seen memories of childish days
When pains and pleasures lightly came and went;
The sympathies of boyhood richly spent
In fearful wanderings through forbidden ways;
The vague, but manly, wish to tread the maze
Of life to noble ends; whereon intent,
Asking to know for what man here is sent,
The bravest heart must often pause, and gaze—
The firm resolve to seek the chosen end
Of manhood's judgment, cautious and mature:
Each of these viewless bonds binds friend to friend
With strength no selfish purpose can secure.

My happy lot is this, that all attend
That friendship which came first, and which shall last
endure.

—Stephen E. Spring Rice

True friendship is a plant of slow growth and must
undergo and withstand the shocks of adversity before
it is entitled to the appellation.

George Washington

All Children Scuff the Leaves

Autumn there never was that did not know
The narrow legs of children, quick or slow,
Scuffing through gutterways the fallen leaves.
The untaught heart receives
This gaudy, simple legend of the year,
For children have no fear
Of what goes down to death
In one fine flame of breath.
Warmed by this red, this gold,
They are not pinched by rumor of the cold.
With such bright ruin billowed at their knees,
They do not look at trees
Naked against the sharpened tongues of air;
And even if they looked, they would not care.

Yet, with a need they do not understand,
Once in a while they take each other's hand.

—Sarah Litsey

Lifelong Friends

Lifelong friends—what lovelier thing
Could the hand of life bestow
Than a friendship built upon
All the precious things you know:
Faith in each other and the ties
Of understanding, old and wise.

A friendship flavored by the past,
Old swimming holes and days
*   shot through*
With loafin', fishin', catching crabs,
The crazy things that small kids do,
A hide-out in the woods somewhere,
Adventure on the bill of fare.

School days and hockey, bikes
    and skates,
A boy's face tangled in your heart,
Your first small job that in some way
Became the groundwork of your start,
The glamour of a high school dance
That seemed all beauty and romance.

These are the ties, the little things
That add up to the kindly sum
Of all that makes the days worthwhile,
The precious memories that become
As strong as hempen rope to bear
The strands of friendship woven there.

Earth holds no greater good, I think,
Than friendship welded link by link.

—Edna Jacques

Old friends are the great blessing of one's latter years.
Half a word conveys one's meaning. They have a memory
of the same events and have the same mode of thinking. I
have young relations that may grow upon me, for my
nature is affectionate, but can they grow old friends?

Horace Walpole

Family

Friends

Home and Friends

Oh, there's a power to make each hour
    As sweet as heaven designed it;
Nor need we roam to bring it home,
    Though few there be that find it.
We seek too high for things close by
    And lose what nature found us,
For life hath here no friends so dear
    As home and friends around us.

We oft destroy the present joy
    For future hopes and praise them
While flowers as sweet bloom at our feet,
    If we'd but stoop to raise them.
For things afar still sweeter are

When youth's bright spell hath
    bound us,
But soon we're taught the earth
    hath naught
    Like home and friends around us.

The friends that speed in time of need,
    When hope's last reed is shaken,
Do show us still that, come what will,
    We are not quite forsaken.
Though all were night, if but the light
    From friendship's altar crowned us,
'Twould prove the bliss of earth was this:
    Our home and friends around us.

—Author Unknown

Through our friends we are made
brothers to all who live.

Elbert Hubbard

My Early Home

Here sparrows build upon the trees,
    And stock dove hides her nest;
The leaves are winnowed by the breeze
    Into a calmer rest;
The blackcap's song was very sweet
    That used the rose to kiss;
It made the paradise complete:
    My early home was this.

The redbreast from the sweetbriar bush
    Dropt down to pick the worm;
On the horse chestnut sang the thrush
    O'er the house where I was born;
The moonlight, like a shower of pearls,
    Fell o'er this "bower of bliss";
And on the bench sat boys and girls:
    My early home was this.

The old house stooped just like a cave,
    Thatched o'er with mosses green;
Winter around the walls would rave,
    But all was calm within;
The trees are here all green again;
    Here bees the flowers still kiss;
But flowers and trees seemed sweeter then:
    My early home was this.

—John Clare

This Place

This is a place where character is built,
A place where great sacrifice
Is made to bring joy to all others;
I call it my paradise.
This is a place where happiness dwells,
Where love has taken abode;
And it offers wide arms of shelter
To feet grown weary of the road.
Square feet will not measure the distance
From the front door to the back;
Its spirit lights eyes of the children—
Windows that brighten the black.
The sign says, "Come in without knocking";
Strangers no longer need roam;
The atmosphere whispers a welcome—
That's how it is with a home.

—June Masters Bacher

Happy is the house that shelters a friend.

Ralph Waldo Emerson

Lines for a Friend's House

God bless this house and all within it.
Let no harsh spirit enter in it,
Let none approach who would betray,
None with a bitter word to say.
Shield it from harm and sorrow's sting,
Here let the children's laughter ring,
Grant that these friends from year to year
Shall build their happiest memories here.

God bless this house and those who love it,
Fair be the skies, which bend above it.
May never anger's thoughtless word
Within these sheltering walls be heard,
May all who rest beside this fire
And then depart, glad thoughts inspire,
And make them feel who close the door,
Friendship has graced their home once more.

God bless this house and those who keep it.
In the sweet oils of gladness steep it.
Endow these walls with lasting wealth,
The light of love, the glow of health,
The calm of peace, the charm of mirth,
Good friends to sit around the hearth,
And with each nightfall perfect rest—
Here let them live their happiest.

—Edgar A. Guest

We

May we be a happy family
Each moment of the day;
May each be a friend to the other
In every sort of way.
Though it takes a lot of planning
And a lot of praying as well,
Though it takes a lot of forgiving
And more patience than tongue can tell,
May we be a happy family
Full of love we all can share
With each and every neighbor
Who seeks our humble fare.

—Phyllis C. Michael

Friendship needs a certain parallelism of life, a community of thought, a rivalry of aim. . . . Friends are born, not made. . . . Intimates are predestined.

Henry Brooks Adams

One, Two, Three

It was an old, old, old, old lady
And a boy that was half past three;
And the way that they played together
Was beautiful to see.

She couldn't go romping and jumping,
And the boy no more could he;
For he was a thin little fellow,
With a thin little twisted knee.

They sat in the yellow sunlight,
Out under the maple tree;
And the game they played I'll tell you,
Just as it was told to me.

It was hide-and-go-seek they were playing,
Though you'd never have known
it to be—
With an old, old, old, old lady,
And a boy with a twisted knee.

The boy would bend his face down
On his little sound right knee,
And he guessed where she
was hiding
In guesses One, Two, Three.

"You are in the china closet!"
He would laugh and cry with glee—

It wasn't the china closet,
But he still had Two and Three.

"You are up in Papa's big bedroom,
In the chest with the queer old key!"
And she said, "You are warm
and warmer;
But you're not quite right," said she.

"It can't be the little cupboard
Where Mama's things used to be—
So it must be in the clothespress,
Gran'ma!"
And he found her with his Three.

Then she covered her face with
her fingers
That were wrinkled and white and wee,
And she guessed where the boy
was hiding
With a One and a Two and a Three.

And they never had stirred
from their places
Right under the maple tree—
This old, old, old, old lady,
And the boy with the lame little knee—
This dear, dear, dear, old lady
And the boy who was half past three.

—Henry Cuyler Bunner

A Boy Needs a Grandpa

A boy needs a grandpa
For man to man talks,
To go hand in hand
On companionable walks,
To fix up his toys
When they no longer go,
To tell him the things
Little boys want to know.

A boy needs a grandpa
To show him the way
To handle a puppy,
To teach him fair play,
To impart bits of wisdom
Learned throughout long years,
That it's no disgrace
For a man to shed tears.

A boy needs a grandpa
To offer his lap;
And if no one is looking,
They take a wee nap,
Each wrapped in an aura
Of love and esteem,
Each smiling gently
At some special dream.

—Eleanor B. Fallis

Our Own

If I had known in the morning
    How wearily all the day
The words unkind would trouble my mind
    That I said when you went away,
I'd have been more careful, darling,
    Nor given you needless pain;
But we vex our own with look and tone
    We may never take back again.

For though in the quiet evening
    You may give me the kiss of peace,
Yet it well might be that never for me
    The pain of the heart should cease!
How many go forth at morning
    Who never come home at night!
And hearts have broken for harsh words spoken
    That sorrow can ne'er set right.

We have careful thought for the stranger
    And smiles for the sometime guest;
But oft for "our own" the bitter tone,
    Though we love our own the best.
Ah! lip with the curve impatient,
    Ah! brow with the shade of scorn,
'Twere a cruel fate were the night too late
    To undo the work of the morn!

—Margaret E. Sangster

The Joy of
Friendship

Claude Monet

The Worth of a Friend

Can you measure the worth
 of a sunbeam,
The worth of a treasured smile,
The value of love and of giving,
The things that make life worthwhile?
Can you cling to a precious minute
When at last it has ticked away?
At the end of a fleeting lifetime,
Who of us dares bid it stay?

Can you measure the worth of tomorrow,
The good that by chance might come;
The heartaches, the joys, and the sorrows,
Each an important one?

Life has a way of demanding,
Right to the very end,
The prize to be sought—understanding;
That comes from the worth of a friend.

Can you measure the value
 of friendship,
Of knowing that someone is there,
Of faith and of hope and of courage,
A treasured and goodly share?
For nothing is higher in value,
Whatever life chooses to send—
We must prove that we, too, are worthy
And equal the worth of a friend.

—Garnett Ann Schultz

The love of friendship should be gratuitous. You ought not to have or to love a friend for what he will give you. If you love him for the reason that he will supply you with money or some temporal favor, you love the gift rather than him. A friend should be loved freely for himself, and not for anything else.

St. Augustine

A Friend or Two

There's all of pleasure and all of peace
  In a friend or two;
And all your troubles may find release
  Within a friend or two.
It's in the grip of the sleeping hand
On native soil or in alien land,
But the world is made,
    do you understand,
  Of a friend or two.

A song to sing and a crust to share
  With a friend or two;
A smile to give and a grief to bear
  With a friend or two;
A road to walk and a goal to win,
An inglenook to find comfort in,
The gladdest hours that we know begin
  With a friend or two.

A little laughter, perhaps some tears
  With a friend or two;
The days, the weeks, the months
    and years
  With a friend or two;
A vale to cross and a hill to climb,
A mock at age and a jeer at time,
The prose of life takes the lilt of rhyme
  With a friend or two.

The brother-soul and the brother-heart
  Of a friend or two
Make us drift on from the crowd apart
  With a friend or two.
For come days happy or come days sad,
We count no hours but the ones made glad
By the hale good times we have ever had
  With a friend or two.

—Wilbur D. Nesbit

I count myself in nothing else so happy
As in remembering my good friends.

William Shakespeare

The Joy of Friendship

The Friendly Way

Oh, I would tread the friendly way,
The lanes where children romp and play,
The hearty road of fellowship
Where brotherhood is found.
I do not want the sterner game
Where life is but a fight for fame,
Nor would I quit the valleys fair
To stand on higher ground.

There is enough of riches here,
Enough of mirth and honest cheer
To balance all the hurt and pain
As time goes speeding by.
And as each day comes to its end,
If I am sure I have a friend,
For greater wealth or greater fame
I shall not give a sigh.

A place to fill and work to do,
Of comrades here a loyal few,
The children glad that I'm their dad—
All that's my treasure store.
A happy home in which to live—
What further has this life to give?
And where's the rich man with his wealth
Who really gathers more?

I would not shrink nor idly stand
Before the tasks which come to hand;
I would not fail in duty's hour.
But once my work is done,
I would be father to my own,
A neighbor in my little zone,
A man among my fellow men,
And friend to every one.

—Edgar A. Guest

From quiet homes and first beginning
Out to the undiscovered ends,
There's nothing worth the wear of winning,
But laughter and the love of friends.

Hilaire Belloc

Another Friend

My heart is always happy
When I truthfully can say
That by the grace of God
I made another friend today.

*There is no better way
In which to use the time we spend
Than just to smile and say hello
And find another friend.*

We cannot have too many
For the courage that we need

If only in the comfort of
A good and kindly deed,

*If only in the counsel
And the words of sympathy
That leave no doubt or question
As to their sincerity.*

And so it always is a day
That has a happy end
When I can tell myself
That I have made another friend.

—James J. Metcalfe

Confession

I've had a habit all my life,
And this I now confess,
Of placing on a pedestal
The friends that I possess.

*I know that it's not practical,
I know that it's not wise,
But still I go on doing it
With stardust in my eyes.*

I've had some disillusionment,
Some disappointments, too;
At times the pedestal has crashed
Despite what I would do.

*But I have found abundant joy,
So much that's sweet and fine;
I treasure it, unwise or not,
This habit that is mine.*

—Hilda Butler Farr

Along the Way

The things I saw along the way
Were all that made the day a day.
I started out
With mighty dreams,
I set about
My hopes and schemes,
And yet a rose upon a stem
Had not a thing to do with them.

I saw some youngsters playing ball;
That wasn't part of it at all.
I even heard
A bobolink,
Or some such bird
As that, I think,
Although my schemes said not a thing
About the way a bird can sing.

And I suspect, in fact I know,
With life itself I'll find it so,
That when it ends,
What I'll recall
Are flowers and friends,
Not schemes at all.
I'll find the things that made life's day
Were little things along the way.

—Douglas Malloch

Day with a Friend

Spring is a robin;
Summer's a rose;
Autumn's a pumpkin;
Winter's the snows.
Without appointment
They all drop in,
Never explaining
Where they have been,

Bringing a package
Of silvery gray
Or a bright ribbon
Of daffodil day.
Such is our friendship;
I know 'tis true;
For all days are lovely
When shared with you.

—June Masters Bacher

A Sudden Bloom

It's knowing others think of you
That brings a sunny hour;
It's knowing that the winter's gone
That brings a sudden flower.

*For warmth and bloom of friendly things
Are never far apart;*

*A combination such as this
Doth make a merry heart.*

Well, then, it won't be long until
A flower blooms without
And sunshine fills each heart within
To bring a spring about.

—June Masters Bacher

The Heart of a Friend

The heart of a friend is a
   wondrous thing,
A gift of God most fair;
For the seed of friendship there
   sprouts and grows
In love and beauty rare.

As the years go by, bringing joy and grief,
We long for one to share;
And that lovely garden in the heart
   of a friend
Proves a shelter from all care.

Bless God for the love of friends
   so true,
A love akin to His,
Which knows our faults and
   loves us still;
That's what real friendship is.

Yes the heart of a friend is a
   wondrous thing,
A gift of God most fair;
May I carefully tend the seed which grows
In friendship's garden there.

—Pat Lassen

When You Know a Fellow

When you get to know a fellow,
    Know his joys and know his cares,
When you've come to understand him
    And the burdens that he bears,
When you've learned the fight
      he's making
    And the troubles in his way,
Then you find that he is different
    Than you thought him yesterday.

You find his faults are trivial
    And there's not so much to blame
In the brother that you jeered at
    When you only knew his name.
You are quick to see the blemish
    In the distant neighbor's style;
You can point to all his errors
    And may sneer at him the while.

And your prejudices fatten,
    And your hates more violent grow
As you talk about the failures
    Of the man you do not know.
But when drawn a little closer
    And your hands and
      shoulders touch,
You find the traits you hated
    Really don't amount to much.

When you get to know a fellow,
    Know his every mood and whim,
You begin to find the texture
    Of the splendid side of him.
You begin to understand him,
    And you cease to
      scoff and sneer;
For with understanding always
    Prejudices disappear.

You begin to find his virtues,
    And his faults you cease to tell;
For you seldom hate a fellow
    When you know him very well.
When next you start in sneering
    And your phrases turn to blame,
Know more of him you censure
    Than his business and his name.

For it's likely that acquaintance
    Would your prejudice dispel,
And you'd really come to like him
    If you knew him very well.
When you get to know a fellow
    And you understand his ways,
Then his faults won't
      really matter,
For you'll find a lot to praise.

—Edgar A. Guest

Living with the People

Living with the people, the good, the brave, the strong,
Glad to pass the time of day with all who come along.
Lord, it's good to meet Your children as they trudge life's thoroughfare
And learn the hopes they cherish and the dreams they see out there.

Living with the people here upon the kindly earth,
And finding in the strangest garb the messengers of mirth,
For many a stirring tale of life the passer-by can tell,
And every man is worth your while if you but know him well.

Living with the people, the rich, the poor, the wise,
The same breeze blowing over them, the same sun in their eyes;
And this you learn from high and low, throughout life's stretch of years.
We're brothers in the joys we take and brothers in our tears.

I'm sorry for the haughty man who holds his head in air
And passes by in cold disdain the garbs of toil and care,
For though he may be rich and great, 'tis lonely he must live;
He misses all the glorious joys his fellows have to give.

Oh, walk with them and talk with them and hear the tales they tell;
The passers-by would be your friends if you but knew them well.
The children of the Lord are they, and as they come and go,
There is not one among them all that is not good to know.

—Edgar A. Guest

Friendship

I want the man I meet each day,
Wherever I may be,
To know that joy and happiness
Just radiate from me.
I want to put so much into
The handclasp I extend
That every man I meet will say,
"I know he'll be a friend."

I want to greet my fellow men
With such a hearty smile
That it will banish all their care
And make life seem worthwhile.

I want to understand their need
And such assistance lend
That every man I know will feel,
"I'm glad he is my friend."

I ask not honor nor reward
For anything I do;
I just would open wide my heart
And let the love shine through.
Though I but meet a brother once,
One touch, one smile I'd send
And cause that man to sing for aye,
"I'm glad he is my friend."

—Francis J. Gable

True friendship speaks with gentle hands
To strengthen one in need,
With loving care and deep concern
As its most special creeds.

Craig E. Sathoff

Letters Between Friends

To a Distant Friend

Why art thou silent! Is thy love a plant
Of such weak fiber that the treacherous air
Of absence withers what was once so fair?
Is there no debt to pay, no boon to grant?

Yet have my thoughts for thee been vigilant,
Bound to thy service with unceasing care—
The mind's least generous wish a mendicant
For naught but what thy happiness could spare.

Speak!—thought his soft warm heart, once free to hold
A thousand tender pleasures, thine and mine,
Be left more desolate, more dreary cold
Than a forsaken bird's nest filled with snow
'Mid its own bush of leafless eglantine—
Speak, that my torturing doubts their end may know!

—William Wordsworth

My Dear Liszt,

I must say, you are a friend. Let me say no more to you, for although I always recognized in friendship between men the noblest and highest relation, it was you who embodied this idea into its fullest reality by letting me no longer imagine, but feel and grasp, what a friend is. I do not thank you, for you alone have the power to thank yourself by your joy in being what you are. It is noble to have a friend, but still nobler to be a friend.

—Richard Wagner

I salute you. I am your friend, and my love for you goes deep. There is nothing I can give you which you have not got; but there is much, very much, that, while I cannot give it, you can take.

No heaven can come to us unless our hearts find rest in today. Take heaven! No peace lies in the future which is not hidden in this present little instance. Take peace! The gloom of the world is but a shadow. Behind it, yet within our reach, is joy! There is radiance and glory in the darkness, could we but see—and to see we have only to look. . . . I beseech you to look.

Life is so full of meaning and purpose, so full of beauty beneath its covering, that you will find earth but cloaks your heaven. Courage then to claim it, that is all! But courage you have, and the knowledge that we are pilgrims together, wending through unknown country, home.

And so, I greet you with profound esteem and with the prayer that for you, now and forever the day breaks, and the shadows flee away.

—Fra Giovanni
1513 A.D.

Dear Mrs. Hewson,

In looking forward, twenty-five years seems a long period; but, in looking back, how short! Could you imagine that it is now a full quarter of a century since we were first acquainted? It was in 1757. During the greatest part of this time, I lived in the same house with my dear deceased friend, your mother; of course, you and I saw and conversed with each other much and often. It is all to our honor that, in all that time, we never had among us the smallest misunderstanding. Our friendship has been all clear sunshine, without any, the least, clouds in its hemisphere. Let me conclude by saying to you what I have had to frequent occasion to say to my other remaining old friends: the fewer we become, the more let us love one another.

Adieu, etc.

—Benjamin Franklin
January 27, 1783

Dear Susie,

Thank the dear little snow flakes, because they fall today rather than some vain weekday when the world and the cares of the world try so hard to keep me from my departed friend. And thank you, too, dear Susie, that you never weary of me, or never tell me so, and that when the world is cold, and the storm sighs e'er so piteously, I am sure of one sweet shelter, one covert from the storm! The bells are ringing, Susie, north, and east, and south, and your own village bell, and the people who love God are expecting to go to meeting. Don't you go, Susie, not to their meeting, but come with me this morning to the church within our hearts where the bells are always ringing; and the preacher whose name is Love shall intercede there for us!

Thank you for my dear letter, which came on Saturday night when all the world was still. Thank you for the love it bore me, and for its golden thoughts, and feelings so like gems that I was sure I gathered them in whole baskets of pearls! I mourn this morning, Susie, that I have no sweet sunset to gild a page for you, nor any bay so blue—not even a little chamber way up in the sky, as yours is, to give me thoughts of heaven, which I would give to you. . . . Yet, Susie, there will be romance in this letter's ride to you—think of the hills and the dales, and the rivers it will pass over, and the drivers and conductors who will hurry it on to you; and won't that make a poem such as ne'er can be written?

—Emily Dickinson
February 1852

Letter of My Thoughts

I've written you in thoughts, my friend,
So often through the years,
But somehow ink just couldn't find
The words to make thoughts clear.

Within my thoughts I have relived
Those happy times we shared
As childhood friends who ran and played
Without the slightest care.

You were a friend to me back then,
And still you are today;

For memories can give us strength
And help us on our way.

In my thoughts I've thanked you friend,
Though surely not enough,
For your example years ago
Still helps when times are rough.

I've often written in my thoughts,
But here at last are words
To say I thank you for the joys
That in my heart you've stirred.

—Craig E. Sathoff

Friends Through Correspondence

I have found that friends who live
One thousand miles away
Have added color to my life
Through written words each day.

They always show more interest
Than those friends along the street
Who do not know my thoughts at all
Though many times we meet.

I've found companionship so dear
Through looked-for envelopes
Containing inspiration of
My deepest dreams and hopes.

I would not trade this priceless gift
For anything on earth,
Because through correspondence I
Have found what friends are worth.

—Elsie M. Farr

True friendship thrives through media
Of touch and sight and speech,
But often in the silent times
It most extends its reach.

Craig E. Sathoff

A World of Friendship

Friendly Things

The world is filled with friendly things
From one end to the other:
A fence, a tree, a garden, and
A kitchen and a mother;
The road that winds beyond the hills
To where the sun is rising;
The letter from the kindly pen
Of someone sympathizing;
The ship that sails across the sea
Unmindful of the weather;

The ring around a finger small
That holds two hearts together;
A dog, a cat, a flower fair;
A dinner invitation;
The sky, the moon, the stars and all;
The beauty of creation.
The world is filled with friendly things
For those who try to find them,
Who look for smiles at every turn
And leave their tears behind them.

—James J. Metcalfe

Beneath these fruit-tree boughs that shed
Their snow-white blossoms on my head,
With brightest sunshine round me spread
Of Spring's unclouded weather
In this sequestered nook how sweet
To sit upon my orchard seat,
And birds and flowers once more to greet,
My last year's friends together.

William Wordsworth

Song of Nature

Atune persists in nature, ever new,
Pervading all, the call: "I am with you."

When night has underscored eternity,
The eyes of heaven smile: "I am with you."

With voices trained from deep antiquity,
The crickets' choir intones: "I am with you."

Enfolding you with their identity,
Soft breezes murmur close: "I am with you."

To each step pledging her fidelity,
Earth gladly echoes back: "I am with you."

Man that would dare deny affinity
With other human beings, who were you?

Afraid to share your proud humanity,
For you the generous vainly sing: "I am with you."

When yet a million stars their silent course pursue,
Timed by that solemn chant: "I am with you."

—Elizabeth Selden

The Little Things

My heart is content with just knowing
The treasures of life's little things:
The thrill of a child when it's snowing,
The trill of a bird in the spring.

My heart is content with just knowing
The worth of each gem in the dews,

The circus is here and I'm going,
The thrill of a new pair of shoes.

My heart is content with just knowing
Fulfillment that true friendship brings;
It fills to the brim, overflowing
With pleasure in life's "little things."

—June Masters Bacher

Humble Things

I love the little humble things
That in my garden grow;
Each volunteer is welcome here,
No matter what I sow.
I do not trample clover vines
Or even pull the weeds;

I never prune the crowded blooms
Or pick and save the seeds.
My garden just reseeds itself
Quite as it chooses to,
Just as the little humble things
In life are prone to do.

—June Masters Bacher

My Friend the Sea

So vast and varied are its charms
That call each day to me;
Such personality it has,
My friend, the restless sea.

*Some days it roars and
        wars with life;
Some days it seems to be
A clear and gentle looking glass
That slumbers peacefully.*

Such hidden treasures
        grace its depth;
Such secrets linger there
That I can't even visualize
The jewels rich and rare.

*So often does it seem to call
To ask me to its side
That it has won me as a friend,
A friend who gives me pride.*

—Craig E. Sathoff

In the Forest

In the forest we can rise above our worldly care;
In the forest we may find tranquility and share
The silence and the secret strength of great and ancient trees—
Sturdy oaks and silver birches, laughing in the breeze.

In the forest we can learn life's lessons if we will—
How to turn towards the sunshine, standing straight and still,
How to be content with slow development and grow
In grace and strength in spite of storms, of wind and frost and snow.

Countless birds and insects seek protection in the tree—
Food and shelter; isn't this true hospitality?
And when winds have stripped the branches of their summer dress,
They survive to show the world new forms of loveliness.

Stately tree! Look down on me and teach me how to be
Strong and wise, to live my days in quiet dignity.
In the forest silences, our petty warfares cease.
In God's own cathedral we discover truth and peace.

—Patience Strong

A Man's Dog

Aman's dog stands by him in prosperity and in poverty, in health and in sickness. He will sleep on the cold ground, where the wintry winds blow and the snow drives fiercely, if only he can be near his master's side. He will kiss the hand that has no food to offer; he will lick the wounds and sores that come in encounter with the roughness of the world. He guards the sleep of his pauper master as if he were a prince. When all other friends desert, he remains. When riches take wings and reputation falls to pieces, he is as constant in his love as the sun in its journey through the heavens. If fortune drives the master forth an outcast in the world, friendless and homeless, the faithful dog asks no higher privilege than that of accompanying him to guard against danger, to fight against his enemies. And when the last scene of all comes, and death takes the master in its embrace, and his body is laid away in the cold ground, no matter if all other friends pursue their way, there by his graveside all the noble dog be found, his head between his paws, his eyes sad but open in alert watchfulness, faithful and true even to death.

—George Vest

I Found Loveliness Today

I found loveliness today
Down along life's broad highway—

Saw its beauty in the trees,
Heard it whisper in the breeze,
Listed it in songbird's trill,
Then again in flowering rill,
Felt its warmth in glad sunshine,
Rhythm caught in swaying pine—

All along life's broad highway
I found loveliness today.

I found loveliness today
Down along life's broad highway—

Beauty within pastures green,
Next in clouds of silvery sheen,
Golden glow at break of day,
Joy in children at their play,
Scented odor of wild rose;
Peace I found where violet grows—

All along life's broad highway
I found loveliness today.

—Carleton Everett Knox

Stop, Look, and Listen

Stop, take time to rest awhile,
The world is rich in lore.
Stop, wait, and know
Earth's precious given store.
Stop, there is so much to find:
White billows of a summer cloud,
Wild birds fluting in the trees,
Great mountains rising
    high and proud.

Look, the world is filled
   with varied things
And worthwhile things to see:
Broad fields of waving grain,

Cows grazing on the lea.
Look, watch the butterflies
Serenading every flower;
A waterfall, a giant oak,
And steeples on a tower.

Listen, be still and wait,
You'll hear all kinds of things:
A moth up on the windowpane,
Whir of wild birds on the wing.
Listen, be still and hear
The language of the wildflowers.
Be serene and patient; wait
For new sounds every hour.

—Mamie Ozburn Odum

What a thing friendship is, world without end!

Robert Browning

The Inspiration of Friendship

The Friend Who Just Stands By

When trouble comes your soul to try,
You love the friend who
    just "stands by."
Perhaps there's nothing he can do—
The thing is strictly up to you.
For there are troubles all your own
And paths the soul must tread alone,
Times when love can't
    smooth the road
Nor friendship lift its heavy load.

But just to know you have a friend
Who will "stand by" until the end,
Whose sympathy through all endures,
Whose warm handclasp is
    always yours—
It helps, some way, to pull you through,
Although there's nothing he can do.
And so with fervent heart you cry,
"God bless the friend who
    just 'stands by!'"

—B. Y. Williams

A Mile with Me

Oh, who will walk a mile with me
Along life's merry way?
A comrade blithe and full of glee,
Who dares to laugh out loud and free
And let his frolic fancy play,
Like a happy child through
    the flowers gay
That fill the field and fringe the way
Where he walks a mile with me.

And who will walk a mile with me
Along life's weary way?
A friend whose heart has eyes to see
The stars shine out o'er
    the darkening lea
And the quiet rest at the end
    of the day—
A friend who knows and dares to say
The brave, sweet words that
    cheer the way
Where he walks a mile with me.

With such a comrade, such a friend,
I fain would walk till journey's end,
Through summer sunshine,
    winter rain,
And then, farewell, we shall
    meet again!

—Henry van Dyke

Discovering a Friend

If sorrow never happened
    And trouble never came,
The only thing you'd know about
    Your neighbor is his name.
If all your days were bright and fair
    And certain was your place,
You'd only know a fellow
    By the features of his face.
Acquaintances upon this earth
    Are all you'd ever own
If care had always passed you by
    And grief you'd never known.

Time was I used to nod to one
    Who lived across the way.
I knew his name, and he knew mine;
    We passed the time of day.
But nothing did he mean to me
    And nothing I to him

Until one morning sorrow came
    And all my world was grim.
I saw his face; I felt his hand
    And knew he'd come to lend
The strength I needed, and right then
    I found I had a friend.

'Tis not in sunshine friends are made,
    But when our skies are gray;
The splendid souls that men possess
    Are never on display.
We cannot tell what lies behind
    The hasty nod or smile
Or what of worth will come from it
    In just a little while.
We only know that when we face
    The cares that life must send,
We realize the passer-by
    Has changed into a friend.

—Author Unknown

Friendship that flows from the heart cannot be frozen by adversity, as the water that flows from the spring cannot congeal in winter.

James Fenimore Cooper

To a Friend

You entered my life in a casual way
    And saw at a glance what I needed;
There were others who passed me or met me each day,
    But never a one of them heeded.
Perhaps you were thinking of other folks more,
    Or chance simply seemed to decree it.
I know there were many such chances before,
    But the others—well, they didn't see it.

You said just the thing that I wished you would say,
    And you made me believe that you meant it;
I held up my head in the old gallant way
    And resolved you should never repent it.
There are times when encouragement means such a lot
    And a word is enough to convey it;
There were others who could have, as easy as not—
    But, just the same, they didn't say it.

There may have been someone who could have done more
    To help me along, though I doubt it;
What I needed was cheering, and always before
    They had let me plod onward without it.
You helped to refashion the dream of my heart
    And made me turn eagerly to it;
There were others who might have (I question that part)—
    But, after all, they didn't do it!

—Grace Strickler Dawson

When to the Sessions of Sweet Silent Thought

When to the sessions of sweet silent thought
I summon up remembrance of things past,
I sigh the lack of many a thing I sought
And with old woes new wail my dear time's waste.
Then can I drown an eye (unus'd to flow)
For precious friends hid in death's dateless night,
And weep afresh love's long since cancell'd woe,
And moan th' expense of many a vanish'd sight.
Then can I grieve at grievances foregone
And heavily from woe to woe tell o'er
The sad account of my fore-bemoaned moan,
Which I new pay as if not paid before.
But if the while I think on thee, dear friend,
All losses are restor'd and sorrows end.

—William Shakespeare

To a Friend

I ask but one thing of you, only one,
That always you will be my
      dream of you;
That never shall I wake to find untrue
All this I have believed and rested on,
Forever vanished, like a vision gone
Out into the night. Alas, how few
There are who strike in us a
      chord we knew
Existed, but so seldom heard its tone;
We tremble at the half-forgotten sound.
The world is full of rude awakenings
And heaven-born castles shattered
      to the ground,
Yet still our human longing vainly clings
To a belief in beauty through all wrongs.
Oh stay your hand, and leave my
      heart its songs!

—Amy Lowell

The Making of a Friend

We nodded as we passed each day
And smiled and went along our way.
I knew his name, and he knew mine,
But neither of us made a sign
That we possessed a common tie;
We barely spoke as we passed by.

How fine he was I never guessed.
The splendid soul within his breast
I never saw. From me were hid
The many kindly deeds he did.
His gentle ways I did not know,
Or I'd have claimed him long ago.

Then trouble came to me one day,
And he was first to come and say
The cheering words I longed to hear.
He offered help, and standing near
I felt our lives in sorrow blend—
My neighbor had become my friend.

How many smiles from day to day
I've missed along my narrow way.
How many kindly words I've lost;
What joy has my indifference cost?
This glorious friend that now I know
Would have been friendly years ago.

—Author Unknown

We cannot tell the precise moment when a
friendship is formed. As in filling a vessel drop
by drop, there is at last a drop which makes it
run over; so in a series of kindnesses there is at
last one which makes the heart run over.

Samuel Johnson

I Saw in Louisiana a Live Oak Growing

I saw in Louisiana a live oak growing,
All alone stood it and the moss hung down from the branches,
Without any companion it grew there uttering joyous leaves of dark green,
And its look, rude, unbending, lusty, made me think of myself,
But I wondered how it could utter joyous leaves standing alone there
    without its friend near, for I knew I could not,
And I broke off a twig with a certain number of leaves upon it,
    and twined around it a little moss,
And brought it away, and I have placed it in sight of my room.
It is not needed to remind me of my own dear friends
(For I believe lately I think of little else than of them),
Yet it remains to me a curious token, it makes me think of manly love;
For all that, and though the live oak glistens there in Louisiana solitary
    in a wide flat space,
Uttering joyous leaves all its life without a friend a lover near,
I know very well I could not.

—Walt Whitman

Lost and Found

I missed him when the sun began to bend;
I found him not when I had lost his rim;
With many tears I went in search of him,
Climbing high mountains which did still ascend
And gave me echoes when I called my friend;
Through cities vast and charnel houses grim,
And high cathedrals where the light was dim,
Through books and arts and works without an end,
But found him not—the friend whom I had lost.
And yet I found him—as I found the lark,
A sound in fields I heard but could not mark;
I found him nearest when I missed him most;
I found him in my heart, a life in frost,
A light I knew not till my soul was dark.

—George Macdonald

*Those friends thou hast, and their adoption tried,
grapple them to thy soul with hoops of steel.*

William Shakespeare

Friends

If all the sorrows of this weary earth—
The pains and heartaches of
    humanity—
If all were gathered up and given me,
I still would have my share of
    wealth and worth
Who have you, Friend of Old,
    to be my cheer
Through life's uncertain fortunes,
    year by year.

Thank God for friends, who dearer grow
    as years increase;
Who, as possessions fail our hopes
    and hands,
Become the boon supreme,
    than gold and lands
More precious. Let all else, if must
    be, cease;
But Lord of Life, I pray on
    me bestow
The gift of friends, to share
    the way I go.

—Thomas Curtis Clark

My Thanks For Others

O Lord, how very much I owe
To others whom you've let me know
   And see from day to day—
The young, the old, the in-between
Who make an entrance in the scene
   In which I'm called to play.

Another's sweet approving smile
Can make my efforts seem worthwhile
   And crown my will to try.
Encouragement another speaks
Is oft the spur my spirit seeks
   Though not quite knowing why.

And, yes, I am so grateful, too
For those who hold a dimmer view
   Of me and my poor part
Because they challenge me to test
What's truly noble, pure, and best
   Within my mind and heart.

I often wonder how I'd be
Without the folks surrounding me—
   My vital, living hem.
That's why I pause to give this prayer
To You it pleased to put them there.
   I thank you, Lord, for them.

—Margaret Rorke

Old and Faithful Friends

To an Old Friend's House

It's never far to an old friend's house,
And the way is smooth and fine;
The path bears many a telltale mark
Of footprints, his and mine.
Each hill and vale and winding curve
Its youthful fancies lends,
And miles are short when I go forth
To the house of an old, old friend.

The day is always bright and fair
When I, on a friend, do call,
Who has been a friend in time and stress
And "stood by" through it all.
Though skies are drear and clouds
*   hang low,*
And the outlook's drab and gray;
There's a radiant glow at an
*   old friend's house*
That drives the gloom away.

Time never drags at an old friend's
    house,
And the hours are filled with joy.
He pictures me, I picture him
As a carefree, laughing boy.
Old faces beam with wrinkled smiles,
And the long years brightly blend
In a wealth of treasured memories—
At the house of an old, old friend.

—Adam N. Reiter

Gathering Up the Threads

How good it is to meet old friends
And gather up the threads once more,
To reminisce of days gone by
And travel through youth's open door.
To stir some cherished memories
Long hidden deep within the heart,
Which never seem to come to life
When traveling down the years apart.
There's nothing more that is as sweet
Or helps to make the spirit soar
As meeting with some good old friends
To gather up the threads once more.

—Hilda Butler Farr

Time Sifts Our Friendships

Time sifts our friendships and our friends,
For time alone can be the test;
And with the passing of the years
We lose the false and keep the best.

And when beyond the distant hills
The golden sun of life descends,
We find God's greatest gift has been
The love of true and faithful friends.

—Patience Strong

Shake Hands

Shake hands, we shall never be friends, all's over;
I only vex you the more I try.
All's wrong that ever I've done or said,
And naught to help it in this dull head:
Shake hands, here's luck, good-bye.

But if you come to a road where danger
Or guilt or anguish or shame's to share,
Be good to the lad that loves you true
And the soul that was born to die for you,
And whistle, and I'll be there.

—A. E. Housman

Remembering

How many, many springtimes
Have come and gone away;
But each one left a memory—
And memories will stay.

How many, many friendships
Life's path has let me see;
I've kept a scrap of each of them
To make the whole of me.

—June Masters Bacher

A Legacy

Friend of my many years!
When the great silence falls, at last, on me,
Let me not leave, to pain and sadden thee,
    A memory of tears,

But pleasant thoughts alone
Of one who was thy friendship's honored guest
And drank the wine of consolation pressed
    From sorrows of thy own.

I leave with thee a sense
Of hands upheld and trials rendered less—
The unselfish joy which is to helpfulness
    Its own great recompense;

The knowledge that from thine,
As from the garments of the Master, stole
Calmness and strength, the virtue which
        makes whole
    And heals without a sign;

Yea more, the assurance strong
That love, which fails of perfect utterance here,
Lives on to fill the heavenly atmosphere
    With its immortal song.

—John Greenleaf Whittier

The True Friend

The true friend stands ever ready to heed every call for help, but never intrudes; and when his mission has been fulfilled, he silently withdraws, always mindful and respectful of the sanctity of the divine heritage of freedom of those whom he befriends.

The true friend helps without any thought of personal praise or profit, not that he may aggrandize and immortalize himself in the hearts of the people, but that he may fulfill the law of righteousness.

To the true friend, it matters not whether those he serves are grateful or ungrateful—he just moves about, doing good for good's sake only. Faithfulness is the guiding principle of the true friend.

—Harry Halsey Starrett

A Cup of Tea

Nellie made a cup of tea,
Made and poured it out for me,
And above the steaming brew
Smiled and asked me, "One or two?"
Saucily she tossed her head;
"Make it sweet for me," I said.

*Two sweet lumps of sugar fell
Into that small china well,
But I knew the while I drained
Every drop the cup contained.
More than sugar in the tea
Made the beverage sweet for me.*

This to her I tried to say
In that golden yesterday—
Life is like a cup of tea
Which Time poureth endlessly,
Brewed by trial's constant heat,
Needing love to make it sweet.

*Then I caught her looking up,
And I held my dainty cup
Out to her and bravely said,
"Here is all that lies ahead;
Here is all my life to be—
Will you make it sweet for me?"*

That was years ago, and now
There is silver in her brow.
We have sorrowed, we have smiled,
We've been hurt and reconciled,
But whatever had to be,
She has made it sweet for me.

—Author Unknown

The Thousandth Man

One man in a thousand, Solomon
    says,
Will stick more close than a brother.
And it's worthwhile seeking him
    half your days
If you find him before the other.
Nine hundred and ninety-nine depend
On what the world sees in you,
But the Thousandth Man will
    stand your friend
With the whole round world against
    you.

'Tis neither promise nor prayer nor show
Will settle the finding for thee.
Nine hundred and ninety-nine of 'em go
By your looks, or your acts, or your glory,
But if he finds you and you find him,
The rest of the world don't matter;
For the Thousandth Man will sink or
    swim
With you in any water.

You can use his purse with no more talk
Than he uses yours for his spendings,
And laugh and meet in your daily walk
As though there had been no lendings.
Nine hundred and ninety-nine
    of 'em call
For silver and gold in their dealings;
But the Thousandth Man he's
    worth 'em all,
Because you can show him your
    feelings.

His wrong's your wrong, and his right's
    your right,
In season or out of season.
Stand up and back it in all men's sight—
With that for your only reason!
Nine hundred and ninety-nine can't bide
The shame or mocking or laughter,
But the Thousandth Man will
    stand by your side
To the gallows' foot and after!

—Rudyard Kipling

Love and Friendship

Love is like the wild rose-briar;
Friendship is like the holly-tree—
The holly is dark when the rose-briar blooms,
But which will bloom most constantly?

The wild rose-briar is sweet in spring;
Its summer blossoms scent the air.
Yet wait till winter comes again
And who will call the wild briar fair?

Then scorn the sill rose-wreath now
And deck thee with the holly's sheen,
That when December blights thy brow
He still may leave thy garland green.

—Emily Brontë

True Friendship No Season Knows

A friend is like a mighty oak
When all its leaves are gone;
A friend is like a single note
When other birds have flown.

A friend is like the broad expanse
Of shady summer green;
A friend is like the autumn bronze
That lends a later sheen.

A friend is like an evening song
Heard in the twilight hush;
A friend is one who says, "Come in,"
When others seem to rush.

For friendship true no season knows
And oft ignores the clock;
It lends a hand to strangers
And stretches round the block.

—June Masters Bacher

Old and Faithful Friends

155

Salt of the Earth

New friends I cherish
And treasure their worth,
But old friends to me
Are the salt of the earth.
Friends are like garments
That everyone wears—
New ones are needed
For dress-up affairs;
But when we're at leisure,
We're more apt to choose
The clothes that we purchased
With last season's shoes.

Things we grow used to
Are the ones we love best—
The ones we are certain
Have weathered the test.
And isn't it true,
Since we're talking of friends,
That new ones bring pleasure
When everything blends?

But when we want someone
Who thinks as we do
And who fits, as I said,
Like last summer's shoe,
We turn to the friends
Who have stuck through the years,
Who echo our laughter
And dry up our tears.
They know every weakness
And fault we possess,
But somehow forget them
In friendship's caress.

The story is old,
Yet fragrant and sweet.
I've said it before,
But just let me repeat:
New friends I cherish
And treasure their worth,
But old friends to me
Are the salt of the earth.

—Author Unknown

New Friends and Old Friends

Make new friends, but keep the old;
Those are silver, these are gold.
New-made friendships, like new wine,
Age will mellow and refine.
Friendships that have stood the test—
Time and change—are surely best;
Brow may wrinkle, hair may gray,
Friendship never knows decay.
For 'mid old friends, tried and true,
Once more we our youth renew.
But old friends, alas! may die;
New friends must their place supply.
Cherish friendship in your breast—
New is good, but old is best.
Make new friends, but keep the old;
Those are silver, these are gold.

—Joseph Parry

Friendship is something you consider for a moment, but cherish for an eternity.

Tim Traynor

Art Credits

Cover: Henry Hubert La Thangue, *In the Orchard*. **Page 5:** Pierre-Auguste Renoir, *Dance at the Moulin de la Galette*, 1876, Musée d'Orsay, Paris. **6:** Edouard Manet, *Clematis in a Crystal Vase*, c. 1881, Musée d'Orsay, Paris. **9:** Sir James Guthrie, *Midsummer*, Royal Scottish Academy, Edinburgh/Bridgeman Art Library, London. **13:** Pierre-Auguste Renoir, *Alfred Sisley and His Wife*, c. 1868, Wallraf-Richartz-Museum, Cologne. **17:** Mary Cassatt, *Portrait of Lydia Cassatt*, Museum of the Petit-Palais, Paris. **18:** Edouard Manet, *The Conservatory*, 1878-79. **22:** Henri Eugene Le Sidanier, *Les Arbres Fleuris Gerberoy*, Christie's, London. **25:** Mary Cassatt, *The Loge*, 1882, Chester Dale Collection, © 1995 Board of Trustees, National Gallery of Art, Washington. **27:** Pierre-Auguste Renoir, *Young Girls at the Piano*, c. 1890, Musée du Louvre, Paris/Bridgeman Art Library, London. **28:** James J. Tissot, *The Croquet Player*, Private Collection/Bridgeman Art Library, London. **31:** Joaquin Sorolla, *Promenade on the Beach*, Sorolla Museum, Valencia. **32:** Pierre-Auguste Renoir, *Claude Renoir Playing*, c. 1905, Musée de l'Orangerie, Paris. **34:** Edouard Manet, *The Old Musician*, 1862, Chester Dale Collection, © 1995 Board of Trustees, National Gallery of Art, Washington. **35:** Mary Cassatt, *The Sisters*, c. 1885. **36:** Claude Monet, *Woman with a Parasol—Madame Monet and Her Son*, 1875, Collection of Mr. and Mrs. Paul Mellon, © 1995 Board of Trustees, National Gallery of Art, Washington. **39:** Pierre-Auguste Renoir, *La Lecture*, Musée du Louvre, Paris. **43:** Mary Cassatt, *Young Women Picking Fruit*, c. 1891, Oil on Canvas, 130.8 x 90.2 cm, The Carnegie Museum of Art, Pittsburgh, Patrons Art Fund, 22.8. **45:** Mary Cassatt, *Children on the Beach*. **49:** Claude Monet, *The Artist's Garden at Vétheuil*, 1880, Ailsa Mellon Bruce Collection, © 1995 Board of Trustees, National Gallery of Art, Washington. **54:** Mary Cassatt, *The Family*, c. 1892, The Chrysler Museum of Art, Norfolk, Virginia; gift of Walter P. Chrysler, Jr., 71.498. **57:** Pierre-Auguste Renoir, *Gabrielle and Jean*, c. 1895, Musée de l'Orangerie, Paris. **63:** Claude Monet, *The Women in the Garden*, 1866-67, Musée d'Orsay, Paris. **67:** Pierre-Auguste Renoir, *Umbrellas*, National Gallery, London. **68:** Pierre-Auguste Renoir, *The Swing*, 1876, Musée d'Orsay, Paris. **71:** Pierre-Auguste Renoir, *After Lunch*, Stadelisches Institute of Art, Frankfurt, Germany. **72:** Alfred Sisley, *Orchard in Spring*, 1881, Museum Boymans-van Beuningen, Rotterdam. **80:** Pierre-Auguste Renoir, *La Grenouillère*, 1869, Pushkin Museum of Fine Arts, Moscow/Bridgeman Art Library, London. **85:** Edouard Manet, *Peonies in a Vase*, c. 1864, Musée d'Orsay, Paris. **86:** Eugene Boudin, *The Beach at Trouville*. **90:** Pierre-Auguste Renoir, *Woman with a Letter*, 1894, Musée de l'Orangerie, Paris. **93:** Pierre-Auguste Renoir, *Coco Writing*. **94:** John Singer Sargent, *Breakfast in the Loggia*. **103:** Claude Monet, *Green Reflexion* (detail), c. 1916-26, Musée de l'Orangerie, Paris. **106:** Peter Severin Kroyer, *Summer Evening on the Skagen South Beach* (detail), Skagens Museum, Denmark/Bridgeman Art Library, London. **108:** Harry Watson, *Morning in the Woods*, Oldham Art Gallery, Lancs/Bridgeman Art Library, London. **111:** Mary Stevenson Cassatt, *Susan on a Balcony Holding a Dog*, c. 1880, Oil on Canvas, 39½ x 25½ in (100.33 x 64.77 cm), in the collection of the Corcoran Gallery of Art, Museum Purchase, Gallery Fund. **117:** Pierre-Auguste Renoir, *Mixed Flowers in an Earthenware Pot*, bequest of John T. Spaulding, courtesy of Museum of Fine Arts, Boston. **120:** Alfred Sisley, *The Builder's Yard at Matrat, Moret-sur-Loing*, c. 1883, Musée départementale de l'Oise, Beauvais. **125:** Edouard Manet, *At Père Lathuille's*, 1879, Musée des Beaux-Arts de Tournai. **126:** Edouard Manet, *The Reading*, 1869, Musée d'Orsay, Paris. **129:** Claude Monet, *Terrace at Sainte-Adresse, Near La Havre*, Metropolitan Museum of Art, New York/Bridgeman Art Library, London. **134:** Claude Monet, *La Barque*, Musée d'Orsay, Paris. **140:** Alfred Sisley, *The Canal du Loing à St. Mammès*, 1885, Philadelphia Museum of Art, Mr. and Mrs. Carroll S. Tyson Collection. **143:** William Stewart Macgeorge, *Sloe Blossom*, Smith Art Gallery and Museum. **144:** Mary Cassatt, *Woman with a Red Zinnia*, 1891, Chester Dale Collection, © 1995 Board of Trustees, National Gallery of Art, Washington. **150:** Mary Stevenson Cassatt, *Five O'Clock Tea*, M. Theresa B. Hopkins Fund, courtesy of Museum of Fine Arts, Boston. **152:** Edouard Manet, *The Balcony*, 1868, Musée d'Orsay, Paris. **156:** Pierre-Auguste Renoir, *Dance at Bougival* (detail), 1883, Picture Fund, courtesy of Museum of Fine Arts, Boston. **159:** Pierre-Auguste Renoir, *Spring Bouquet*, 1866, courtesy of The Fogg Art Museum, Harvard University Art Museums, bequest of Grenville L. Winthrop.

Photography Credits

All floral arrangements from the book *A Cascade of Flowers* by Jane Newdick, photography by Di Lewis, © 1990 by Salamander Books Limited, published by Salamander Books Limited, London.

Photography of fine art supplied by Art Resource; The Carnegie Museum of Art; The Chrysler Museum of Art; The Corcoran Gallery of Art; Harvard University Art Museums; Museum of Fine Arts Boston; National Gallery of Art; Philadelphia Museum of Art; and Superstock, Inc.